FALSE SECURITY

False Security

B. VINCENT

CONTENTS

| 1 |

Introduction

Who wouldn't want a little extra security with their investment funds? Whether it's a multi-million-dollar payday or $5 worth of Dogecoin, we all seek financial peace of mind. However, when it comes to passive investments, that sense of security might be more elusive than we realize. The true cost of holding a portion of your portfolio in cash can be difficult to discern during market surges. Still, the price of missed opportunities can be more corrosive than you may think—even when short-term risks appear low. It's self-evident that the logical end of every investment process is, indeed, an investment; we invest to build a future.

The Complacency Trap

Unfortunately, many investors fall into a complacency trap, assuming that strong past performance of a passive investment is predictive of future success. This belief extends not only to general market performance but also to the viability of passive investments in individual companies. Devaluing passive investing as an unsophisticated strategy oversimplifies the issue. Not all wide-moat businesses are necessarily good investments at their current market capitalizations.

The Rise of Retail Traders

Since late 2019, major zero-fee brokerages have documented an accelerating pace of net new customer acquisitions. This surge has led to a disquieting disconnect between dangerously naive retail traders who believe they are employing "passive investment strategies" and the fundamentals that actually make such strategies wise.

Gatekeepers and Passive Strategies

It may benefit gatekeepers who receive fee uplifts to accommodate all passively managed inflows, much like preferring a boat that rows itself. A passive strategy involves positioning capital in a cost-efficient package of all the world's publicly tradeable businesses, offering an illusion of security that may not hold up under scrutiny.

A Deeper Dive

In this book, we'll delve into the misconceptions and pitfalls of passive investing. We'll explore how seemingly safe strategies can sometimes lead to missed opportunities and overlooked risks. By examining the nuances of the investment landscape, we'll uncover why a more active, informed approach may be necessary to truly secure your financial future.

| 2 |

Understanding Passive Investments

A passive investment is a method of generating income using investment strategies that require minimal action from the investor. These strategies involve purchasing investments designed to be held over the long term, focusing on maximizing returns without the need for frequent trading. Unlike day traders or news-driven investors, passive investors adhere to a "buy-and-hold" approach, allowing their investments to grow over time. This strategy is closely associated with index investors who aim for market returns without inflating investment costs.

Types of Passive Investment Approaches

There are various passive investment approaches, including:

- **ETFs/Index Funds**: Funds that track market indices, providing broad market exposure.
- **Sector Funds**: Focused on specific industry sectors.
- **Market Cap Index Funds**: Investments based on the market capitalization of companies.
- **Dividend Funds**: Investments in companies that pay regular dividends.

- **Balanced Funds**: A mix of stocks and bonds to balance risk and return.
- **Lifecycle Funds**: Designed to adjust the asset mix as the investor approaches retirement.
- **ESG and SRI Funds**: Investments that consider environmental, social, and governance criteria.
- **Global Funds**: Investments in international markets.
- **Income Funds**: Focused on generating regular income for investors.

Benefits of Passive Investments

- **Low Costs**: Reduced fees and transaction costs.
- **Consistent Long-Term Gains**: Steady returns over an extended period.
- **Overall Market Exposure**: Broad diversification across the market.
- **Low Risk**: Reduced volatility compared to active trading.
- **Ease of Operation**: Simplicity in managing investments.

Drawbacks of Passive Investments

- **No "Beating the System"**: Inability to outperform the market through short-term strategies.
- **Market-Dependent Performance**: Reliance on overall market trends.
- **Potential for Amplified Returns**: Higher concentration risk if many investors follow the same strategy.
- **Liquidity Risks**: Potential for liquidity issues during market downturns.

Definition and Types

At an entry-level, investment discussions often revolve around two main types: passive and active. Many modern investors, including those in cryptocurrency and stock options, incorporate passive investments into their portfolios. These investments are characterized by minimal daily contribution once acquired, focusing on historical performance rather than potential future returns.

Active Investments: In contrast, active investments involve deliberate selection and frequent trading based on performance prospects. This approach aims to outperform market averages through strategic buying and selling.

Benefits and Drawbacks

Passive investments offer significant advantages but also come with certain drawbacks. They capitalize on market momentum with fewer transactions, often referred to as "inception trades" by economists Eduardo Dávila and Cecilia Parlatore. However, high market participation in passive strategies can reduce diversity and amplify returns, leading to potential value loss and liquidity issues during regular rebalancing.

Advantages:

- Low transaction costs.
- Steady, long-term growth.
- Broad market exposure.
- Simplicity and ease of management.

Disadvantages:

- Inability to outperform the market.
- Dependence on market performance.
- Risk of reduced diversity.
- Potential liquidity issues.

In Conclusion

Understanding the dynamics of passive investments is crucial for any investor. While they offer simplicity and long-term gains, it's essential to be aware of their limitations and potential risks. By recognizing the benefits and drawbacks, investors can make informed decisions that align with their financial goals.

| 3 |

The Rise of Passive Investing

The inception of passive investing as we know it can be traced back to the mid-1970s when it emerged as an alternative to traditional active management. It quickly captured the interest of academics and individual investors who were skeptical of professional money managers' ability to generate superior returns. Although passive investment methods existed in earlier decades, the modern incarnations of the passive portfolio and the indexed mutual fund did not debut until 1975 and 1976, respectively.

Historical Context and Key Drivers

The shift away from active investing was driven by the consistent and visible underperformance of individual stocks and bonds compared to broad diversified market benchmarks. Investors started to realize that actively managed funds often failed to outperform the market, making passive investing an attractive alternative.

Two major factors enabled passive investing to gain popularity:

1. **Development of the Shareholding Base:** The expansion of the nation's shareholding base allowed ordinary individual investors to own stocks more easily. Before the 1970s and early 1980s, only very wealthy families, mutual funds,

and pension funds could afford to invest in the stock market. The democratization of stock ownership was pivotal in popularizing passive investing.

2. **Decline in Informational Advantage**: The informational advantage of active managers diminished due to a series of deregulatory initiatives, such as the Investment Company Act of 1940. This legislation aimed to prevent another stock market crash but also led to an oligopolistic investment industry with limited need for investment advice beyond what firms could offer. The decline in the informational edge of active managers made passive investing more appealing to investors.

The End of the "Nifty Fifty" Era

The rise of passive investing coincided with the end of the "Nifty Fifty" craze. From 1973 to 1974, at the peak of their popularity, investors heavily speculated on a handful of "one-decision" stocks—companies deemed so solid that they were considered buy-and-hold-forever investments. However, the overvaluation of these stocks, some with P/E ratios exceeding the ten-year rule proposed by Francis Schaeffer, highlighted the risks of active stock-picking and reinforced the appeal of passive investing.

Transition to Modern Passive Strategies

The transition to modern passive strategies marked a significant shift in investment philosophy. Indexed mutual funds, introduced in the mid-1970s, allowed investors to match the performance of market indices rather than attempting to outperform them. This approach provided a cost-effective way to achieve broad market exposure and minimize the risks associated with active management.

Impact on Investment Industry

The rise of passive investing transformed the investment industry, leading to increased transparency and lower costs for investors. As more individuals embraced passive strategies, the demand for index funds and exchange-traded funds (ETFs) surged, further solidifying the dominance of passive investing in the financial markets.

In Conclusion

Understanding the rise of passive investing provides valuable insights into the evolution of investment strategies. The shift from active to passive management was driven by the need for consistent returns, cost efficiency, and broader market access. By recognizing the historical context and key drivers, investors can appreciate the benefits and limitations of passive investing in today's financial landscape.

| 4 |

Common Misconceptions

Despite the rising popularity of passive investment vehicles like index funds and ETFs, some investors remain skeptical about their effectiveness compared to active management. Critics of passive investing often argue against it by highlighting perceived limitations and contrasting it with "active" strategies. Let's address some of these common misconceptions.

Misconception 1: Passive Investing is Pointless

A frequent argument against passive investing is the notion that there is no need to pay someone to simply put money into the S&P 500 index. This perspective oversimplifies the value of passive investing. The reality is that the S&P 500 index has consistently provided a reliable way to capture the superior economic performance of the U.S. market with relatively low risk.

Misconception 2: Active Opportunities are Superior

Another popular misconception is that passive investing prevents investors from accessing the most exciting and innovative securities. Critics often advocate for active opportunities, suggesting they offer better returns. However, this ignores the consistent performance of passive investments over time. While active investments may occasionally outperform, they often do so at the cost of higher risk and fees.

The Reality of Market Performance

Understanding the history of stock market performance in the U.S. reveals the folly of these misconceptions. The S&P 500 index, for example, has demonstrated resilience and growth despite economic downturns. During the 2008 Great Recession, the index dropped about 40%, but it rebounded the following year, highlighting its long-term stability. Stocks are inherently volatile due to supply and demand, economic conditions, and unpredictable events. This volatility is a natural aspect of investing, regardless of the strategy.

The Consistency of Passive Investing

Passive investing focuses on long-term growth and market exposure without the need for frequent trading. This approach minimizes costs and reduces the risks associated with active management. The performance of passive investments, like the S&P 500 index, showcases their ability to deliver steady returns over time. Despite market fluctuations, the overall trend has been upward, making passive investing a viable strategy for many investors.

Economic Insights

Complex economic concepts explain why these misconceptions are misleading. Passive investing offers broad market exposure, low costs, and reduced risk, which are appealing attributes for many investors. The long-term benefits of passive strategies outweigh the short-term allure of active trading, especially when considering historical performance data.

In Conclusion

Addressing these common misconceptions is crucial for understanding the true value of passive investing. While active strategies may seem appealing, the consistent performance, low costs, and reduced risk associated with passive investments make them a strong contender for long-term financial growth. By recognizing the realities of market performance and the benefits of passive strategies, investors can make more informed decisions about their financial future.

| 5 |

Risk Factors in Passive Investments

Due to the vast number of potential passive investments, the indexes they track are constantly changing, contributing to market volatility. As the economy evolves, funds must buy new assets and sell others to stay aligned with the updated index. For instance, in 2021, Tesla quickly rose to become one of the most valuable companies in the S&P 500. This rapid rise led many investors to jump in, causing the stock to become overvalued. Consequently, Tesla's shares began to trade sideways until it was eventually removed from the index. This scenario underscores how changes in index composition can lead to overvaluation and subsequent price corrections.

Technical Investing Strategies

Technical investing strategies often rely on historical price data to identify potential buying and selling points. Passive investments typically buy stocks when they are added to an index and sell them when they are removed. This approach can result in lower demand from retail investors and reduced liquidity between these events, potentially accentuating any downtrends.

Lack of Active Management

Passive funds do not have an active manager who can respond to significant drops in security prices by actively investing in assets expected to outperform the market. Instead, they are programmed to buy and hold the securities in their index. A notable example of this was during the market selloff in March 2020. The magnitude and speed of the selloff caused some passive funds to freeze redemptions, preventing investors from panic selling. Other funds faced significant tracking errors as the drop in value of some securities led to restrictions on new borrowing. This forced them to sell other holdings to meet redemptions, further impacting the value of stocks still trading in the fund.

Market Volatility

One of the primary risks associated with passive investments is market volatility. Passive investment vehicles closely mimic the market index they track. If that underlying index fluctuates widely, the value of the investment follows suit. Historical data shows that market volatility is the rule rather than the exception. For instance, from mid-2007 to 2009, the S&P 500 experienced a dramatic loss of nearly 50%. This volatility not only led to substantial dollar losses on investment values but also a significant decline in potential dividend income. Many investors sold shares to stop their losses, not realizing that those who sold when stock prices were at their lowest lost the most. This reactionary behavior is known as "buy high and sell low," a sure path to investment losses.

In effect, the passive investor has opted for an "asset allocation" fund with a blind "buy and hold" strategy. When a drop in portfolio value and dividend income is combined with a poorly diversified investment structure (meaning a substantial part of savings is concentrated in one asset class), the ability to retire at age 60 might be compromised. Hyperactive concentration and lack of diversification invite disaster from unforeseeable future events and cause most investors to sell out due to a lack of tolerance for market fluctuations. Preventing such a reaction requires a well-diversified portfolio, something contrary to the passive investor doctrine.

Lack of Active Management

A major characteristic of passive investment is the absence of active management, which leads to significantly lower management expenses. However, this comes with certain downsides. Instead of focusing on allocation and active management, a passive fund manager concentrates merely on the quantity and features of the assets in the chosen index. There is no need for active trading to switch the fund's structure, which can result in potential negative implications associated with passive management. The fund's portfolio is created once at the beginning and remains unchanged until the end of its existence. Yet, a passive investor observing a decreasing market value may feel a strong urge to reconsider the fund's composition.

There are limitations set for such operations. A passive fund or unit-stock company is recognized by investors as a mechanism to replicate the return on a chosen benchmark. The fund's return is managed to align with the benchmark, minimizing tracking errors. Investors in such funds usually exit after a period of low or negative performance. Thus, while passive investing involves minimal active trading by fund managers, it can lead to active trading by investors themselves. If a passive investor is unprepared for quick price drops and starts hastily selling portfolio assets, this might coincide with a market low, exacerbating losses.

In Conclusion

Understanding the risk factors associated with passive investments is crucial for making informed financial decisions. Market volatility, the absence of active management, and the inherent challenges of index tracking can all impact the performance of passive funds. By recognizing these risks, investors can better navigate the complexities of passive investing and develop strategies to mitigate potential downsides.

| 6 |

Case Studies of Passive Investment Failures

Case Study: Black Monday

The October 1987 stock market crash, known as Black Monday, serves as a stark example of the risks associated with passive investments. Leading up to the crash, the yield on the 10-year U.S. Treasury bond rose steadily as investors reacted to the prospects of skyrocketing inflation and eroding purchasing power due to a weaker U.S. dollar. This was a reaction to the U.S. Congress voting to raise the debt ceiling. The resulting selling frenzy drove bond yields 120 basis points lower by October 20, 1987. Despite movements in various market components, the Dow Jones Industrial Average (DJIA) continued its downward trajectory throughout the week, culminating in the crash on Black Monday.

The Crash

On October 19, 1987, the DJIA plummeted by 22.61% in a single day—a catastrophic drop that took many investors by surprise. Those who had passively invested in U.S. Treasuries may have believed they had sufficiently diversified their portfolios to shield against stock market volatility. However, the so-called "safe-haven" of U.S. Treasuries fell by 4.66% on the same day. This unexpected drop in Treasury values highlighted the limitations of relying solely on passive strategies for diversification.

Impact on Bond Futures

To underscore the extent of the financial turmoil, the long bond futures fell by 9.7% on Black Monday. Even with futures exchanges initially limiting the movement in U.S. Treasury 30-year bond futures to 2 points per day, the restriction was lifted on October 20, causing the long bond futures to drop by 17.7% in just two days. The mere anticipation of an increased interest rate spread between long-term Treasury bonds and Dow constituents significantly drove down Treasury prices, demonstrating the interconnectedness of market components and the challenges in hedging against such widespread market failures.

Lessons Learned

The Black Monday crash reveals several critical lessons for investors relying on passive strategies:

- **Diversification Limits**: Simply holding a diversified portfolio of passive investments does not guarantee safety from market volatility. The correlation between different asset classes can lead to simultaneous declines, undermining the perceived security.
- **Market Interdependence**: Financial markets are highly interconnected, and events affecting one sector can have cascading effects on others. Passive investors must understand that external economic factors can significantly impact their portfolios.
- **Lack of Active Management**: Passive investments lack the proactive adjustments that active management can provide. In times of market distress, the absence of an active manager to navigate volatility can result in substantial losses.

In Conclusion

The Black Monday crash is a powerful reminder of the inherent risks in passive investing. While passive strategies offer benefits like lower costs and broad market exposure, they are not immune to extreme market events. By recognizing these risks and understanding the limitations of passive strategies, investors can make more informed decisions and consider incorporating a blend of passive and active management to mitigate potential drawbacks.

| 7 |

Strategies for Mitigating Risks in Passive Investm

Dylan and Kimberly's findings suggest that investors can shield themselves against some risks associated with passive investments by diversifying their portfolios across a broad range of geographic regions and industries. "After all," they write, "the main advantage of the low-cost indexing strategy is arguably the portfolio-level diversification it offers." Diversification can help reduce losses when specific markets or industries experience downturns, though it may come with its own set of challenges.

Complementing Passive Strategies with Vigilance

To reduce exposure to the dangerous reliance on mindless, greedy, or panic-driven stock movements, investors should complement their passive strategies with a posture of acute watchfulness. These strategies encourage at least annual monitoring of market conditions underpinning low-risk stock tournaments created by indexing. Institutions that advertise passive products have an obligation to ensure individuals are actively monitoring their investments. Fortunately, many retail investors already exhibit this vigilance, actively managing their portfolios despite holding 'safe' stocks.

Investors can also impose their own discipline by getting rid of stocks or entire funds when circumstances change and moving into new investments that will perform better in current conditions. This active approach can ensure that a portfolio is 'reset' and operating based on current fundamentals.

Diversification

Diversification is a key risk mitigation tool in investment, and it is particularly important for passive funds. By spreading investments across different factors—such as geographic regions, industries, and asset classes—investors can minimize exposure to risk. This approach reduces the likelihood that all investment options or assets will be negatively impacted simultaneously.

Passive funds often track markets, with indices defined in various ways (e.g., market capitalization-weighted). Individual investors, firms, and public institutions can protect their investment value by incorporating diversification into their broader strategy. It should be noted that diversification does not necessarily increase value or prevent losses, but it increases the likelihood of favorable future outcomes given various market conditions. From a risk perspective, diversification affects the portfolio's covariance structure, division of returns, and variance.

For example, with 12 industry sectors defined by the Global Industry Classification Standard (GICS) system within the Russell 1000, an investor applying an equal weight diversification strategy would have about 8.33% of their portfolio exposed to risk in each sector. Alternatively, they could invest more heavily in certain sectors like information technology and healthcare, and less so in others like real estate and consumer staples.

Regular Monitoring and Rebalancing

Even with no active management, regular monitoring and rebalancing are crucial to maintaining the desired asset mix. Passive fund managers should monitor each asset at least once a year to ensure the portfolio remains aligned with its goals. Over time, changes in market conditions can cause the portfolio to deviate from its original allocation.

Having a clear goal in mind can signal when to rebalance the portfolio. Although market developments may change the desired weightings, an investor might wish to increase exposure to appreciating assets (e.g., real assets) while managing regulatory constraints and potential tax implications.

Rebalancing helps maintain the portfolio's risk profile and ensures that it remains aligned with the investor's financial objectives. By regularly adjusting the asset allocation, investors can mitigate the impact of market volatility and other external factors.

In Conclusion

Mitigating risks in passive investments requires a combination of diversification, regular monitoring, and rebalancing. By spreading investments across different regions, industries, and asset classes, investors can reduce their exposure to specific risks. Complementing passive strategies with vigilance and periodic adjustments helps maintain the portfolio's alignment with financial goals and market conditions. Understanding these strategies allows investors to navigate the complexities of passive investing and achieve long-term financial success.

| 8 |

Conclusion

In this essay on the false sense of security in passive investments, I have argued that while passive investments are often lauded for their ability to provide individuals with average or above-average returns at low cost and high efficiency, they also harbor several significant drawbacks that are frequently overlooked. Two primary negatives are the flawed belief in market efficiency and the misconception that the rewards of active investments do not justify their costs.

Market Efficiency and Latent Risk

The assumption that markets are perfectly efficient and that passive investments will always outperform is fundamentally flawed. Everyday investors often cannot trade as frequently or as effectively as market dynamics might suggest. This results in latent risk and, arguably, fragility within their portfolios. Additionally, this can lead to a mismatch between an investor's portfolio and their time preference for risk, potentially jeopardizing their financial goals.

Collective Moral Hazard

Moreover, passive investments embed a form of collective moral hazard. While individual investors might avoid speculation, the large pool of investors within a passive investment fund cannot escape the negative consequences. This collective behavior can invite adverse outcomes, such as diminished social trust and a weakened sense of community and continuity. The broad implications of relying solely on passive investments can undermine the preservation and continuation of what investors hold dear.

Balancing Active and Passive Strategies

In conclusion, while passive investments are widely used globally by diverse individual investors and organizations, it is crucial to recognize the potential risks and misconceptions they carry. Achieving a balanced approach that incorporates both active and passive strategies can help mitigate these risks. Active management can provide the necessary adjustments during market fluctuations, while passive strategies offer cost efficiency and broad market exposure. By being mindful of the false sense of security that passive investments can create, investors can make more informed decisions and secure their financial futures more effectively.

| 9 |

References

1. "Physical ownership: You can take it with you." Discusses three primary methods of investing in gold: buying physical gold, purchasing shares of gold mining companies, and buying shares in a fund that holds physical gold bullion. Each method has its own advantages and disadvantages.

2. "Survey: MFs that track index expected to see highest inflows." Reports on three fund houses in India—Kotak, IDBI, and Gold—that offer ETFs replicating broad-based indices, with notably low expense ratios of 0.80%.

3. Ontario's mandatory pension plan: Analyzes how benefit statements, retirement projections, and commuted value reports are based on low-risk government bond rates. Highlights potential insufficiencies in generating real returns to protect against inflation and longevity for annuities and Life Income Funds (LIFs).

4. "Robo-Advisors - Not As Simple And Easy As They Seem." Explores how Robo-Advisors use capital-weighted combinations of Exchange Traded Funds (ETFs) to maintain low trading costs and Management Expense Ratios (MERs). Notes the high correlation in investment mixes among different Robo-Advisors and the common use of 3-5% cash to keep Strategic Asset Allocation steady during volatile markets.